The
ARABIAN DESERT

A Chronicle of Contrast

The
ARABIAN DESERT

A Chronicle of Contrast

John Carter

IMMEL
Publishing

The Arabian Desert
Designed and produced by Cigale Limited
for IMMEL Publishing, Suite 903, Kaki Center,
Medina Road, Jeddah, Saudi Arabia and
34 Stansfield Road, London SW9 9RZ, UK
First published 1983

Phototypeset in Monophoto Palatino by
MS Filmsetting Limited, Frome
Somerset, England
Printed and bound in Japan by
Dai Nippon Printing Co, Tokyo

British Library Cataloguing in Publication Data

Carter, John R. L.
    The Arabian Desert
    1. Arabian Desert—Description and travel
    I. Title
    915.3′045   DS207

ISBN 0 907151 06 X

Photographic acknowledgements
All photographs listed on a page are from the same
organisation or individual unless otherwise credited.

Aramco, Dhahran: 11, 20–21, 35, 90 (below), 91
(below), 95 (below), 107 (below)

John Carter: 22–23, 43 (below), 47 (below), 62
(below left & right), 63 (top right), 66 (top), 67, 80
(below), 90–91 (top), 92, 93 (top), 107 (top)

Keith Collie: 81 (top)

James Doran: 2–3, 32–33, 40–41, 44 (top), 60, 84
(centre), 85

Ministry of Information, Riyadh: 59, 80 (top)

Dr Angelo Pesce: 4–5, 16–19, 24–25, 34, 38–39,
44 (below), 46–47 (top), 50–56, 57 (below), 58,
72, 78–79, 82–83, 84 (top), 88–89, 94 (below)

Jill Silsby: 36 (top)

Julian Sutton: 1, 6, 12–15, 26–31, 36 (below), 37,
41 (inset), 42, 43 (top), 46 (below), 48–49, 57
(top), 61, 62–63 (top), 63 (centre, below left &
right), 64–65, 66 (below), 68–71, 73–77, 81
(below), 84 (below), 86–87, 93 (below), 94 (top),
95 (top), 96–105, 106, 108–112

Map & diagram artwork: Ian Stephen

Page 1: *A solar powered telephone on the Tabuk road,
north of Medina, demonstrates one of man's most recent
impressions on the vast spaces of the desert.*

Pages 2 & 3: *Western man's traditional view of the
desert is exemplified by this dune near Sakaka in Jawf,
which is about seventy metres high.*

Pages 4 & 5: *Parallel dunes in the south of the
Peninsula roll into infinity, shrouded in a suitably
mysterious light.*

Contents

Introduction

The passage of geological time always seems more easy to measure than to comprehend. It is difficult to conceive what it means when we learn that the world is about five billion years old. Indeed, older men are startled to find that the tiny length of their own lifetime, as far as the younger generation is concerned, seems to be rooted in an earlier historical period. So perhaps it is with the ancient primordial rocks, because deserts are actually quite young. The world had deserts some two hundred and thirty million years ago in the Permian period, but these no longer exist; and though geology tells us that there are signs of aridity in our present desert areas going back about sixty-three million years, the evidence of botany places the date of the creation of the modern desert only one to five million years ago. It is extraordinary to think that all the animals and plant species which one sees in the dry areas, all adapted so multifariously and cleverly to their arid environment, have evolved in this comparatively short space of geological time.

The most important factor leading to the creation of a desert region is the removal of cloud cover. When one considers that around ninety-five percent of all clouds evaporate into invisible vapour and never part with a drop of water, it is perhaps surprising that there are not more deserts. Those we have in the world today have been caused by a complex mixture of geographic and climatic factors which have led to a diminution of the cloud cover. The world revolves at the equator with a speed of twenty-five thousand miles in twenty-four hours, whereas at the poles there is no movement; as this revolving takes place the atmosphere circulates in a reasonably well defined series of giant swirls. The air in the equatorial and swifter moving part tends to be hotter and so moves in a generally upward direction. This rising air flows north and south from the equator, where it has created an area of low pressure, and descends in the sub-tropical zones creating high pressure. It thereupon repeats this pattern to produce high pressure again at the poles. The areas subject to low pressures are the ones which, in general, get the most rainfall. The desert regions are located in areas of high pressure where the descending air picks up moisture instead of dropping it. This basic picture is modified by the position of the continental land masses as well as the seasonal tilting of the earth in relation to the sun.

This very general picture is finished off by the positioning of mountain ranges which lie around the desert areas. These ranges accept such precipitation of moisture as may be available with very little, if any, left for the land beyond.

When all these factors act in concert to form a desert, one is not faced with a *fait accompli*. Desert landscape is as subject to change as any other, but here the forces of erosion act in a different way. Land-forms in a humid area are subject to erosion which is directed towards sea level and the erosion itself is restrained by the growth of vegetation. In humid regions the land tends to be sharply cut in the beginning of the process reaching maximum relief of its features later, in maturity, and wearing down in old age to a level plain dotted with isolated mountain remnants. Desert areas on the other hand attain their period of maximum relief at the initial stage of their development and maturity and old age are both marked by an evening out of the landscape relief. Eventually the mountains are reduced to small lumps called inselbergs which resemble islands sitting on the plain or remain as crumbling pillars. Eventually even these will disappear but so far none of the deserts have reached this stage and perhaps they never will because climatic changes could well interrupt the cycle, as could alterations in the earth's crust.

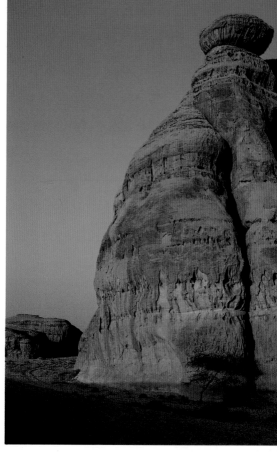

Above: *This shrine-like rock in the Northern Hijaz was formed by centuries of remorseless erosion.*

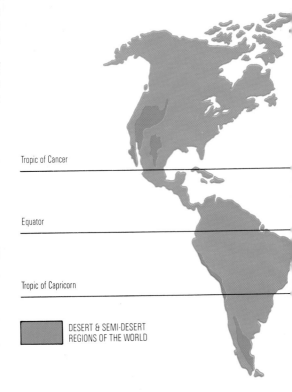

Tropic of Cancer

Equator

Tropic of Capricorn

DESERT & SEMI-DESERT REGIONS OF THE WORLD

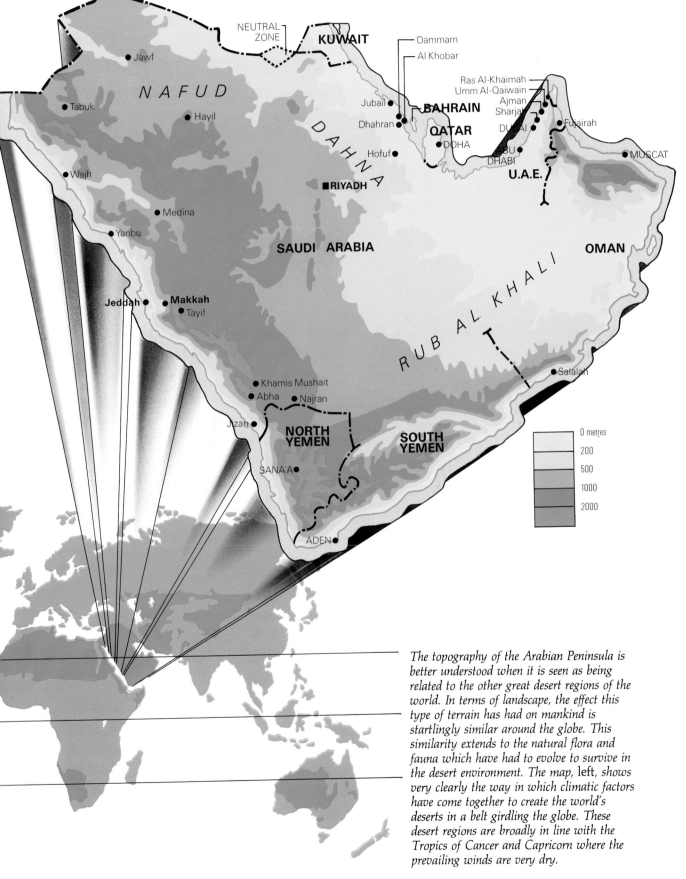

The topography of the Arabian Peninsula is better understood when it is seen as being related to the other great desert regions of the world. In terms of landscape, the effect this type of terrain has had on mankind is startlingly similar around the globe. This similarity extends to the natural flora and fauna which have had to evolve to survive in the desert environment. The map, left, shows very clearly the way in which climatic factors have come together to create the world's deserts in a belt girdling the globe. These desert regions are broadly in line with the Tropics of Cancer and Capricorn where the prevailing winds are very dry.

7

THE ARABIAN DESERT

Badanah

NEUTRAL ZONE

Sakakah
Jawf
Rafha
KUW

Qaysumah
Ras Al Khafji

NAFUD
Tabuk

Tayma
Hayil

DAHNA

Mada'in Salih
Al-Ula
Buraydah
Khurais

Wajh
Khaybar
NAJD
Diraiyah

Umm Lajj
RIYADH ■

Dawadimi

Medina
Afif
Al Kharj

Yanbu

HIJAZ
Masturah

Wadi
Fatima
Jeddah
Makkah
Sulayyil

Tayif

RED
SEA
HIJAZ
Lith
Bishah

Qunfudhah
ASIR

Abha
Khamis
Mushait

Najran

Jizan

NORTH
YEMEN

SANA'A

Hodeidah

8

ADEN

The Geology of the Peninsula

The delight for a geologist in a desert area such as the Arabian Peninsula is that the geology is immediately apparent. Scoured and eroded to its bare bones, the skeleton of the world is plain for all to see. In general, the areas associated with the great sands of the Nafud, Dahna and Rub' al Khali coincide with the areas of Quaternary derivation. The western part of the Peninsula, which is very largely Pre-Cambrian, is characterised by the remains of volcanic activity, both craters and lava flows. In the east lie the bulk of the important oil deposits whose wealth has contributed to the taming of the desert.

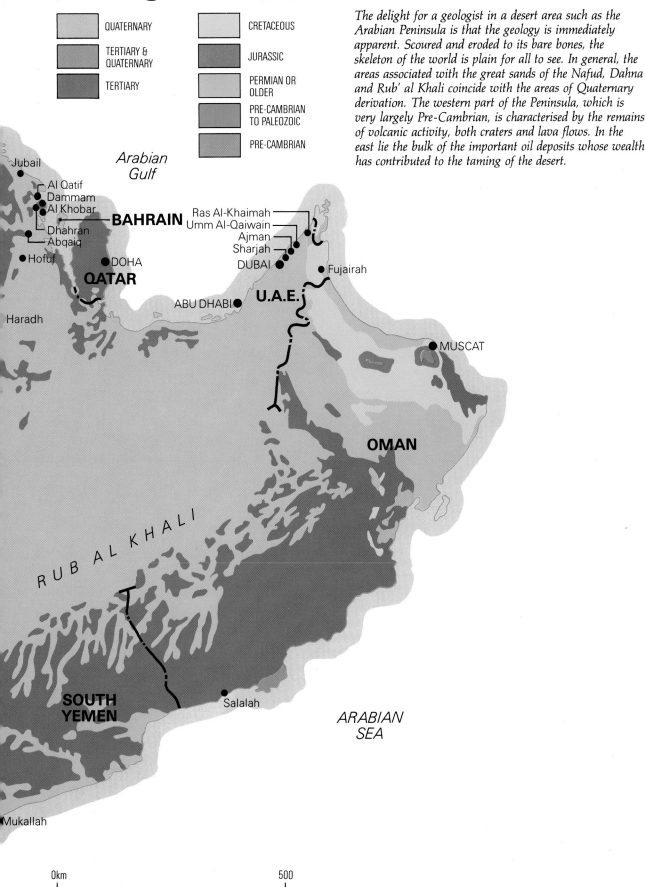

QUATERNARY

TERTIARY &
QUATERNARY

TERTIARY

CRETACEOUS

JURASSIC

PERMIAN OR
OLDER

PRE-CAMBRIAN
TO PALEOZOIC

PRE-CAMBRIAN

Arabian
Gulf

Jubail
Al Qatif
Dammam
Al Khobar
Dhahran
Abqaiq
Hofuf
QATAR
DOHA
Haradh

BAHRAIN

Ras Al-Khaimah
Umm Al-Qaiwain
Ajman
Sharjah
DUBAI
Fujairah

ABU DHABI
U.A.E.

MUSCAT

OMAN

R U B   A L   K H A L I

**SOUTH
YEMEN**
Salalah

*ARABIAN
SEA*

Mukallah

0km   500

9

The main agent of erosion is usually water and the wind is of secondary importance. However, in the arid areas there is not much of the former and the wind has an unimpeded passage to play with the product of such water erosion as there is. Its dehydrating effect also ensures that its freedom is not constrained by the growth of vegetation. The wind performs its part in the formation of the desert landscape in two ways. Firstly, it sculpts the rocks by carrying sand about. However, in this respect it rarely raises the sand more than a few feet into the air; dust is a very different matter, and results in erosion close to ground level producing bizarre effects. Soft sandstone is undercut and curious mushroom shapes are produced. Harder materials are polished, sometimes almost like gems. However, it is the second function of the wind to create what has become the classical picture of the desert—the dunes. In fact, of course, sand dunes only cover a very small part of the landscape we call desert. Most of the desert landscape is bare gravel plain.

It may be thought that the haphazard blowing of the wind following a chaotic course would pile up sand in an irregular fashion, but this is not so. Sand dunes are surprisingly regular in shape and possess some precise definition despite their initial appearance to the casual observer. The most easily recognised, and perhaps the most common, is the barchan dune. This is often quite small and is the typical crescent-shaped dune which often occurs in groups, rather like a family. The second form of dune looks somewhat like a whale and is called a longitudinal dune.

In desert regions, only about ten per cent of the sun's rays are prevented from reaching earth by clouds and particles of dust in the air. Similarly, the lack of cloud cover enables almost all the day's accumulated heat to escape to the upper air at night.

The barchan is found in places where there is a scarcity of sand and a predominant wind direction, the regular shape being due to the blown grains passing over the horns more easily than they can over the centre of the crescent. Longitudinal dunes are also formed where there is a predominant wind direction and a larger supply of sand. The barchans can reverse their shape if the wind direction changes and they can move across the desert floor some fifty feet or more in a year.

When there is no predominant wind direction the forms taken by the dunes become more complex and star shaped dunes are made. These are not so mobile as the barchans, indeed they may not move at all and so they become a permanent part of the landscape. In Saudi Arabia the longitudinal dune is a feature of the Dahna sands and the desert areas towards the southern Gulf and Oman. Barchans are found almost everywhere in open areas where they walk across new roads and building sites. Star shaped dunes reaching heights of some seven hundred feet are mainly found in the great desert areas called the Empty Quarter. Here too one sees a Sand Sea which occurs when sand dunes form on top of other, older dunes.

Right: An oil company truck lumbers through the expanse of the Rub' al Khali.

The principal dune types are illustrated below. Red arrows indicate the predominant direction of the wind.

Moderate winds produce transverse dunes.

Longitudinal dunes result from stronger winds.

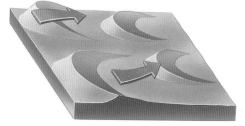

A relative paucity of sand causes barchans.

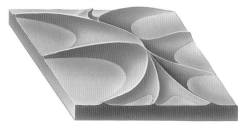

Star dunes are static in spite of the wind.

The sand itself is of great interest and at once poses the question as to where all those billions of tons have come from. As sand is made up of almost spherical balls of quartz, sandstone itself must be a minor source. It would seem that the major source is the tiny quartz crystals found in hard igneous rocks. These have broken off and, though it used to be thought that they would have been shaped by water, attain their spherical shape by being blown about in the wind and colliding with each other. When the round shape is reached the sand grain may retain it for millions of years. To achieve the same effect through water erosion would take too long and it has been estimated that such a grain would have to be washed fifty times round the world before it became round in shape. Abrasion by the wind would get the same result almost a thousand times faster.

One of the strangest properties of the dunes is their ability to make a quite extraordinary noise. No one has yet thought out an explanation for this, but occasionally large volumes of sand slip down the side of a large dune and produce a deep and resonant booming sound. After the first fall there are often others on neighbouring dunes. The resultant effect is both eerie and striking as the booms reflect from one another and create the impression that someone is beating an enormous gong. The heavily vibrating noise continues for some minutes.

But the cause of the other characteristic of the desert which has figured so strongly in desert tales is well known. The mirage occurs due to the bending of light waves as they pass through

The glistening black stone fields in the Northern Hijaz form one of the most formidable desert barriers, even today.

layers of air of differing density. Mirages in the desert are almost always inferior mirages and usually reflect the sky itself. Heat shimmer makes the image seem to move and a plain can appear to be covered with water with lapping waves just like a real lake. Rocky outcrops become islands, bushes and trees become reflected as images at its side. The so-called superior mirage seen at sea, where two images appear, one inverted, are not often encountered in deserts.

The mirage is seen everywhere but the singing sands are only heard in the Empty Quarter or where really large dunes occur. The bedouin generally refer to the phenomenon as *Hanayna* or bellowing, but the two tribes most intimately connected with the great sands of the Empty Quarter each have a special name of their own for it. The Rashid call the phenomenon *al Damam* and the Murra call it *al Hiyal.*

Occasionally the sand can emit other strange sounds; sometimes the pacing of camels over flatter parts of a dune will produce an odd wheezing noise or even a sharp 'phut' as though a stone had struck the sand at high velocity. Vehicle tyres often make an odd wrenching or tearing sound when they start up. Perhaps the strangest property of all, however, is the way in which sand actually seems to melt in the heat of day. Perhaps, too, this has only become apparent with the advent of wheeled vehicles in the desert, but it is a fact that at night and before the sun gets up too high sand will support the tyres of a vehicle when a few hours later it would sink in the same place.

A Chronicle of Contrast

The desert acacia, typical large vegetation of arid areas, provides fodder, shade and fuel to transients and inhabitants alike.

In the Central Hijaz, neither man nor beast, surrounded by intimidating inselbergs, can find comfort in this picture of cruel desolation.

These dunes have a deceptive softness and their voluptuous shapes belie the reality.

Overleaf: *Vast desert spaces such as this daunted the early traveller's heart.*

Salt plaques in the Umm al Sammim of the eastern Empty Quarter form an area of quicksands famous in history for their horror.

Overleaf: *North of Buraydah, spring rains produce an all too impermanent gentleness.*

Above: *Light dunes are blown across the floor of a* wadi *south of Makkah.*

Left: *East of Yanbu, a forlorn thorn tree stands as an illustration that it is possible to survive in rock and sand.*

Right: *The brilliant greens and sickly yellows of the salt bush give visual relief, but even camels eat it only as a last resort.*

Above: *Power lines in the Dahna testify to a less visually grand view of man's activities, but one that will prove more significant in the long term.*

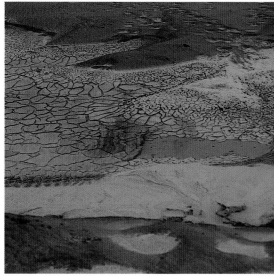

Above: *Erosion, so haphazard, often produces surprisingly regular effects as this solitary inselberg in the Eastern Province shows.*

Overleaf: *In a wadi south of Medina, gentle evening sun and shadows wrap the landscape in a comforting glow.*

Above & right: *Relics of the tortured struggles in the earth's formation abound. The old volcanic crater at Waba, northeast of Tayif, is two kilometres across and 260 metres deep. The crater is no more than a few million years old and may be as young as a few hundred thousand years. A small spring flows down the steep walls where enterprising people have created small gardens. Infrequent heavy rains collect in the bottom of the crater and are dried by the hot sun. Salt leached from the surrounding rocks crystalises and adds a sparkle to the cracked earth.*

Left: *The view from the top of this volcanic cone near Khamis Mushait is typical of the area. Lack of rain and covering vegetation mean that much of the geology lies exposed as it did hundreds of thousands of years ago.*

33

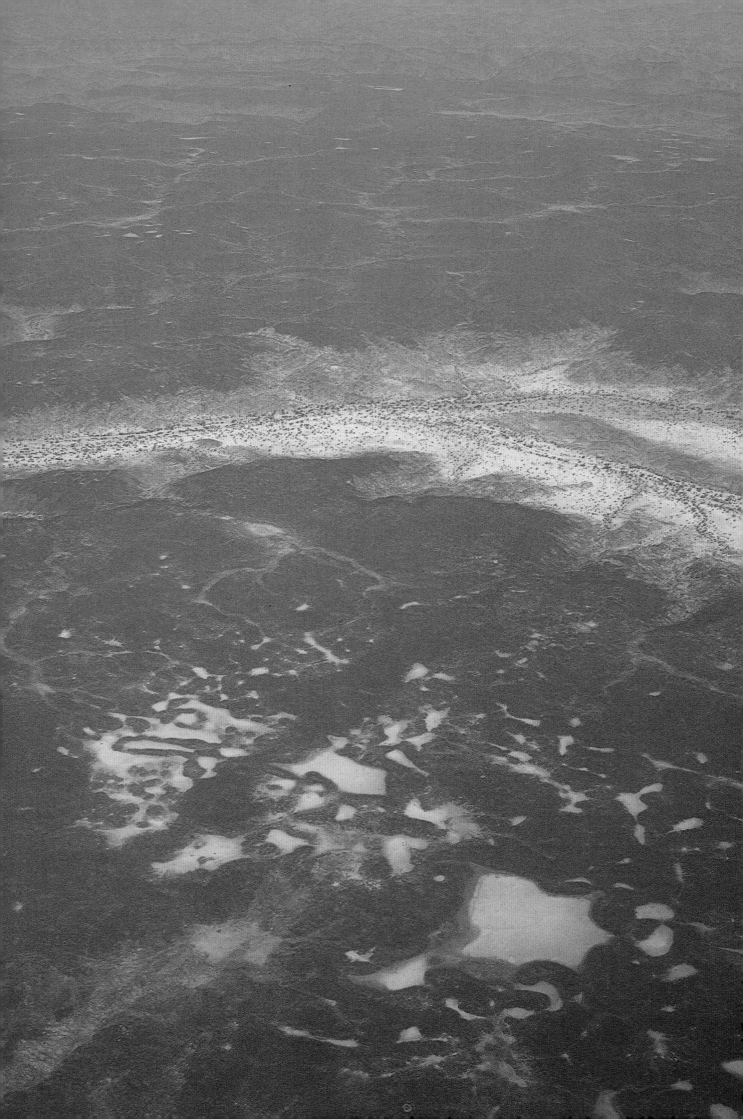

Stark colour contrasts underline the more subtle tones as if to attract the observer's attention. The basalt lava flows at Harrat Rahat (left) and white sands snaking above a black base in the Eastern Province (above) give a wider perspective than may be observed in a shaded wadi *or grey morning sky.*

Top: *Aeons of time have carved these great natural castles on the Tuwaiq Escarpment.*

Above & right: *Sand and water have combined forces to create colourful textures.*

Above: *Millions of grains of sand, acting as nature's sculptors, have slowly formed these stately sentinels which are to be found just outside Hofuf.*

Overleaf: *At the Riyadh-Dhahran-Hofuf crossroads, a solitary rock, shaped like a pepper-pot, surveys a vast scrubby landscape, its hard cap protecting a softer base.*

Man & the Desert

On coming upon the desert for the first time the initial impressions are ones of contrast. The hot day when the taste of dry dust is everywhere is succeeded by such a temperature drop when the sun goes down that the night seems cold. The hotter the day the greater the contrast and the visitor will find himself reaching for a warm woollen jersey or a blanket as the temperature plummets from a hundred and thirty degrees Fahrenheit in the height of summer in the southern sands to about a hundred at night. At the same time the taste of dust goes away, and even if there is no heavy dew the air seems refreshing, carrying a feeling of dampness after the scorching aridity of the day.

The landscape is vast and the traveller will feel that he is able to look over the rim of the horizon itself, feeling perhaps, as well, that he can see to the end of the world. And yet, the only things he sees with real clarity are right under his nose. The little bush has every twig and leaf etched with precise definition. The shape of every stone is memorable and the small beetle burrowing beside it clear in every detail.

The subtle desert colours emerge with the rising sun from what looks like a black and white photograph at night. When there is a good moon the landscape can indeed look like an insufficiently developed photograph. At dawn the rising sun blurs

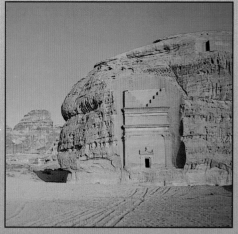

The remains of man's early activity give us only a glimpse of the path he has trod to reach the amazing projects we see today. It is truly a long road from Mada'in Salih (above) *and prehistorical monuments in the northern Hijaz* (below) *to the highways of today and the machines that built them.*

the details at first and then suffuses them for a few minutes in a haze of intimate blues and violets until pinker tones take over and one's field of vision deepens and enlarges. Just before the appearance of the sun itself over the horizon the landscape seems to have a peculiar life of its own and to be expectant, waiting with an almost tangible dread for the heat and torment of another day. Time is itself the contrast here. All these dawn changes take only a few minutes and are ephemeral compared to the hours that follow.

The sky is bigger than anywhere else and a man feels himself to be smaller than he does in any other place.

When the sun is up, and once its orange presence appears on the horizon's rim, one can see it actually moving, so fast does day rush upon the desert. The colours quickly change. Within the hour the black shadows behind rock outcrop, thorn bush and wadi rim melt away as though they were water sucked up and dried. All that is left is the haze and a multiplicity of greys, browns and ochres all of which, by noon, seem to be trying to become white.

In the great sands of the south, in the Dahna and the Nafud, the effect of light is even more dramatic. At night and in the dawn

Top: *Water has been flowing from this Nabatean well at Mada'in Salih for some two thousand years.*

Above: *A bedouin tent at Mada'in Salih represents man's first step in conquering the desert environment.*

Left: *Proud ruins at Diraiyah stand as a monument both to man's endeavour and the ephemeral nature of his works.*

the dunes seem feminine in their langour. The marvellous shapes, curving with delicate grace, make a woman of the landscape. It is the sun which changes all this. Almost charging up the sky it alters the lines of the dunes so they become manly and the glare makes the observer feel he is looking directly into the burnished shield of an ancient warrior.

The sun sets with the same speed and the evening light restores the lady to sight. The stars come out like a blessing, and in the desert they seem very clear and close. Curiously, they also seem far more numerous than elsewhere.

The desert has long inspired the imagination of man. It has often been described as a barrier throughout history. It is therefore humbling for those who describe themselves as civilized to know that for thousands of years it has been a home for many people. People here have been able to construct a way of life that has enabled them to survive from generation to generation, whilst the other branches of mankind on the outside, in the more fertile parts of the world, have written at length about the dangers of what had come to be known as a quite impossible land. The

Above: *In a family tent near Turabah, friendships grow from traditional Arabian hospitality which is, itself, one of the most important factors in surviving harsh desert conditions.*

Left: *Another crucial example of cooperation is the Arab's symbiotic relationship with the camel without which he could not have traversed the desert at all. This partnership was formed about four thousand years ago.*

crossing of the Arabian Peninsula from east to west was a landmark in the history of exploration, but it took place long after the discovery of the sea route around the continent of Africa. European man prided himself on having reached both of the Poles and on having almost conquered Everest before he could make the boast of having crossed the Empty Quarter. And yet, the Arabians had been accomplishing this feat for centuries.

It is true that regularly used routes were first developed to skirt the really difficult regions. However, as long ago as two thousand years before the start of the Christian Era the demands of trade created a route from the ancient kingdoms of south-west Arabia, both directly to the north to reach the Mediterranean in the region of Gaza and to the Gulf coast at Gerrha, somewhere near modern Qatar. It was almost at the beginning of the Christian Era that the first Western incursion into the peninsular was made. A Roman called Aelius Gallus made his disastrous way as far south as Bayhan in an attempt to gain control of the valuable trade in precious gums like myrrh and incense; from then on stories of the impenetrability of Arabia began to be written.

However, the dawn of the Muslim Era some six hundred years later further extended man's ability to cross the desert. The old trade routes were resurrected to form the basis of the roads needed by the pilgrims to perform the Hajj; but in addition, new ones were marked out. The most famous of these followed a route created by the conquering Arab armies on their way to take control of Iraq.

This great route eventually developed into the famous Road of Zubaydah which connected Kufa with the Holy City of Makkah. Wells and way stations were built from the time of the early caliphate but it is the Abbasid Caliphs of Baghdad who must receive most of the credit for a series of very remarkable constructions which made the journey possible almost in comfort for the pilgrims. In particular, Queen Zubaydah, the wife of Harun al-Rashid, did so much for the pilgrims in terms of building rest houses and wells that her name was given to the whole road itself. Whilst the route fell into desuetude during the course of subsequent history, partly because the traffic on it was a lucrative source of plunder to the tribes whose territories bordered the road, it represents a tremendous achievement in the story of man's conquest of the desert. At its peak the route was supplied with more than ninety reservoirs and some one thousand two hundred and thirty wells. Difficult passages were paved and rocks cleared from other parts. In all the Road of Zubaydah extended for over seven hundred miles.

In fact the whole Peninsula was criss-crossed with tracks and paths connecting the centres of settlement, the exact routes they took depending on the availability of wells and the ever precious water. It is only in our own twentieth century that the internal combustion engine has enabled man to loosen his dependence on frequent access to water and to drive paved highways across the desert. Today he can cross the Peninsula in a day, whereas only yesterday it would have taken him many months.

The difficulties of travel, before the conveniences of modern technology transformed desert life, are graphically described by all of the few Westerners who attempted it. Lawrence wrote of it memorably when he said:

> The Fejr Bedouin, whose property it was, called our plain El Houl because it was desolate; and today we rode in it without seeing signs of life; no tracks of gazelle, no lizards, no burrowing of rats, not even any birds. We, ourselves, felt tiny in it, and our urgent progress across its immensity was a stillness or immobility of futile effort. The only sounds were the hollow echoes, like the shutting down of pavements over vaulted places, of rotten stone slab on stone slab when they

tilted under our camel's feet; and the low but piercing rustle of the sand, as it crept slowly westward before the hot wind along the worn sandstone, under the harder overhanging caps which gave each reef its eroded, rind-like shape.

It was a breathless wind, with the furnace taste sometimes known in Egypt when a *Khamsin* came; and, as the day went on and the sun rose in the sky it grew stronger, more filled with the dust of the Nefudh, the great sand desert of Northern Arabia, close by us over there, but invisible through the haze. By noon it blew half a gale, so dry that our shrivelled lips cracked open, and the skin of our faces chapped; while our eyelids, gone granular, seemed to creep back and bare our shrinking eyes. The Arabs drew their head-clothes tightly across their noses, and pulled the brow folds forward like vizors with only a narrow, loose-flapping slit for vision.

Whilst making his first crossing of the Empty Quarter, Thesiger describes what it is like crossing the great sands with camels.

We lead the trembling, hesitating animals upward along great sweeping ridges where the knife-edged crests crumbled beneath our feet. Although it was killing work, my companions were always gentle and infinitely patient. The sun was scorching hot and I felt empty, sick, and dizzy. As I struggled up the slope, knee deep in shifting sand, my heart thumped wildly and my thirst grew worse. I found it difficult to swallow; even my ears felt blocked, and yet I knew that it would be many intolerable hours before I could drink. I would stop to rest, dropping down on the scorching sand, and immediately it seemed I would hear the others shouting, 'Umbarak, Umbarak'; their voices sounded strained and hoarse.

It took us three hours to cross this range.

On the summit were no gently undulating downs such as we had met the day before. Instead, three smaller dune-chains rode upon its back, and beyond them the sand fell away to a salt flat in another great empty trough between the mountains. The range on the far side seemed even higher than the one on which we stood, and behind it were others. I looked round, seeking instinctively for some escape. There was no limit to my vision. Somewhere in the ultimate distance the sands merged into the sky, but in that infinity of space I could see no living thing, not even a withered plant to give me hope. 'There is nowhere to go', I thought. 'We cannot go back and our camels will never get up another of these awful dunes. We really are finished'. The silence flowed over me, drowning the voices of my companions and the fidgeting of their camels.

We went down into the valley, and somehow — and I shall never know how the camels did it — we got up the other side. There, utterly exhausted, we collapsed.

These pictures in words are accounts of quite recent journeys historically and the reader, who nowadays travels with such speed and ease, may not appreciate how new and, perhaps, extra-ordinary, are the facilities he is using. Nowadays too we set out fully expecting to arrive only conceiving the possibility of a puncture to be a possible cause of delay. Our wells are petrol stations and there are no troubles in passing from one to the next. Our petrol-fed camels do not need to spend long hours searching for browse and we sit well insulated from the heat and dust of desert travel. Indeed most of the time modern man avoids the whole thing and simply flies over it all when his closest contact with the harsh realities of the environment only hit him as he struggles into the airport lounge with a heavy suitcase.

Above: *The survival skills of yesteryear continue as the wearer of this* ghutra *shows in protecting himself against the dust.*

A twentieth century camel crosses the Dahna (above) and can penetrate such areas as the Umm al Sammim (left) where no real camel could ever venture.

In the late twentieth century, the fringes of the Dahna provide a playground for man and his dune buggy.

So in these modern days it is not always easy to remember what a very profound effect the impact of the desert has had on forming the lives and lifestyle of all the inhabitants of the Arabian Peninsula. The sparseness of provender for both man and beast created a strong territorial sense on the part of the human beings involved and this itself led to a very profound need for group identity. This was followed in turn by the creation of the tribal system in which groups of people were united by strong family and kinship ties and associated with particular areas of land. The amount of land occupied by any one group was usually just enough to support the group in terms of forage. The group itself tended always to be of a size which was controlled both by the area they occupied and the numbers needed for the successful defence of the area. Naturally, these circumstances required a very definite means of individual identification so that participation in the group could be recognized both by group members and outsiders. The tribes of Arabia thus formed created a complex system of genealogy to accomplish this, a system which continuing into the twentieth century, was first developed many thousands of years ago. The tribal system has been modified by the exigencies of history but only in recent years has the basic need for its existence, namely competition for resources to survive, been in any way overcome. This is what the conquest of the desert means in human terms.

When the groups were formed they were not static organizations. Rather like the sand which made up so much of their environment they were continually being worn into new shapes by the altering relationships they had with other groups. Perhaps the most interesting of these is the relationship between the wandering nomad and the settled man in the villages. It was always an uneasy relationship but the mutual needs of the two groups ensured its continuation. The nomad always had a dependence on the potential bounties of the oasis and the oasis dweller always needed to be defended, as did his communications with other settlements — for it was with them that developing trade could be carried on. Throughout history this simple situation was enlivened by the antagonisms that any competition created. One group would perhaps be successful and increase in size thus needing a larger tribal area to support itself. The extra land could only be acquired at the expense of neighbours who would not unnaturally resist and a war would be the result. The final outcome of the struggle would, however, depend on the ability of the aggressor to hold what he had taken; and always there would be a desire on the part of the loser to regain lost territory. Perhaps, again, one of the groups would be of a size limited to what its area could normally support, but one year there might be little rain, and so the area would be unable to provide sufficient sustenance. In this circumstance the group would be compelled to take to raiding so that pillage would make up the shortfall. Often this would not only be directed against a neighbour, but any source of potential plunder would do. The needs of the moment sacrificing the needs of tomorrow as trading caravans and settlements became the object of attack.

These factors themselves have had a tremendous cultural effect during the course of history. They have provided the background against which the great poets of Arabia composed their best work. An activity which continues to the present day, though it is still best and wonderfully exemplified by the poems known as the *Mu'allaqat* which are tremendous odes composed before the dawn of the Muslim Era. Some small extracts are included here because they form an essential part of the desert

The vivid and tasteful folk art of the desert is beautifully displayed in this camel litter and reflects an ancient tradition to be found in jewellery design and architecture as well as poetic verse.

story and are the human equivalent of the beautiful flowers and vegetation that the desert itself produces, and which form such an enchanting counterbalance to the otherwise harsh environment. The poems themselves are, however, not merely beautiful relics. They also tell us a tremendous amount about the growth of manly ideals and the development of chivalry; a chivalry which in its conception, like so many other things, has had a profound effect on other cultures too.

In one of the seven famous odes, which go to make up the collection known as the *Mu'allaqat*, the poet 'Amr ibn Kulthum, to whose lot it fell to avenge the murder of the poet Tarafa at the hands of the king 'Amr ibn Hind, delivers a most withering challenge of vengeance in high bedouin style.

> With what purpose in view, 'Amr bin Hind,
> do you give heed to our traducers, and despise us?
> With what purpose in view, 'Amr bin Hind,
> should we be underlings to your chosen princelet?
> Threaten us then, and menace us; but gently!
> When, pray, were we your mother's domestics?
> Be sure, that before your time our lances
> baffled our enemies efforts to soften them;
> when the spear vice bit into them, they resisted
> and drove it back like a stubborn, shoving camel,
> a stubborn camel; bend them, and with a creaking
> they strike back at the straighteners neck and forehead.
> Have you been told, regarding Jusham bin Bakr,
> that they ever failed in the ancient's great engagements?
> We are heirs to the glory of Alkama bin Sayf;
> he mastered for us the castles of glory.
> I am heir to Muhalhil and his better,
> Zuhair, a fine treasure indeed to treasure,
> heir to Attab, and Kulthum, the whole of them,
> by whom we attained the heirdom of the noblest,
> heir to Dhul Bura, of whom you've heard tell,
> our defence, through whom we defend the shelterers,
> and, before him, Kulayb the Striver was one of us:
> so what glory is there that we are not possessed of?
> When we tie with a rope our train-camel of battle
> or we break the bond, or the neck of the beast tethered to
>   her.
> We shall be found the firmest of men in duty
> and the truest of men to the oath once taken.
> We on the morn the fire in Khazaz was kindled
> gave succour beyond every other succourer.

Again, 'Imr al Qays in describing 'The Wandering King' evokes a curious tenderness as well as calling up a pointed and accurate picture of the desert itself.

> Halt, friends both. Let us weep, recalling a love and a
>   longing
> by the rim of the twisted sands between al-Dakhul and
>   Hawmal,
> Tudih and al-Mikrat, whose trace is not yet effaced
> for all the spinning of the south winds and the northern
>   blasts;
> there, all about its yards, and away in the dry hollows
> you may see the dung of antelopes spattered like
>   peppercorns.
> Upon the morn of separation, the day they loaded to part,
> by the tribe's acacias it was like I was splitting a colocynth;
> there my companions halted their beasts awhile over me
> saying, "Don't perish of sorrow; restrain yourself decently!"
> Yet the true and only cure of my grief is tears outpoured;
> what is there left to lean on where the trace is obliterated?

To this day the tradition of declaiming poetry is maintained (left) and evokes as much excitement and delight as it ever did.

52

It is due to his poetry perhaps that the bedouin has acquired a romantic image in the West where he is so often described as living an arcadian life. This is an unfair judgement as it ignores the tremendous cost paid by the succeeding generations who really became bedouin from necessity; no one could do so from choice. His air of aristocratic simplicity reinforces this romantic view which forgets the effects of the aching journeys to find water and animal fodder, the frustrations and horror of the sandstorm and the terror of raiders. Against this background he has developed a fierce independence and a striking individualism. These characteristics were forged by his environment and so respected by the Umayyad princes that they sent their sons away from their palaces into the desert to ensure that they learnt the lessons that their people had inherited from the previous centuries of desert life. As the poet made the allusion to the bitter flesh of the colocynth so can we remember the bitter side of desert life, where the human inhabitants of the desert have been as remorselessly formed as the sand grains themselves. Bedouin life and society thus represent a desperate triumph rather than arcadian ease and fatness.

The precious, yet highly formalised, social intercourse of the desert involves the preparation and drinking of coffee and affords a moment of comfort in comparison with the starker reality.

Desert life imposes a strict discipline too. Without it there would be no survival and it underlies all the seeming chaos of history. The outside observer, perhaps not recognising or even ignoring his own historical lessons, often comments on what he sees as a disorderliness in desert society. He fails to notice the tight strings of cohesion which have enabled that society to continue over the centuries; he does not understand that the lack of order he sees is only the music played on the strings and not the strings themselves. The splendid stories of desert life are all about the rules. Heroism and chivalry are all about adherence to the code, cowardice and treachery are a flouting of it.

In the modern world it is difficult at times to see exactly what this means, but it may be that a simple story would describe it. In the twentieth century we take the gratification of many of our needs for granted.

Like coffee, tea is another desert luxury.

Two young desert men rose to their feet when a vehicle drove near the thorn bush in the sands where they were resting in its scant shade. They hailed the vehicle and when it stopped they asked if they could have some water. This was handed out and the men asked the driver if he would honour them by having some tea. He did and they all chatted about this and that for a while. The rules of desert politeness dictated that the guest should drink his tea and have his every need seen to by his hosts before they themselves had anything. After half an hour the driver got back into his vehicle. Just as he was about to let in the clutch and move away the elder of the two bedouin lightly touched his arm and thanked him for the water, adding that they had not had anything to drink for three days. The temperature in the sands was a hundred and thirty at that time of year and it is not difficult to imagine how thirsty the two must have been.

The strings of the rules of hospitality and honour were so strong that they overcame the desperate thirst of the two men who gave no sign of their own suffering as they watched the driver have his tea.

The desert holds a strange sway over those who have lived there. Today, many inhabitants of the new cities recapture earlier memories by taking their weekend picnic on neighbouring dunes.

The life of man in the desert has not only been illuminated by great poetry and sagas of individual courage, heroism and chivalry. There has been time for play as well; perhaps the most famous sporting activity has been falconry.

In Arabia hawking is regarded as being the sport of kings and as a pursuit is mainly followed in northern and north-eastern Arabia. The main game sought is the *hubara* or bustard though both hares and gazelle provide good sport as well. The falcons themselves are caught as they migrate along the coasts of the eastern seaboard. A common method being to peg a pigeon or a jerboa under a wide meshed net set up to slope away from the wind at an angle of about sixty degrees. The falcon will dive at its prey down and into the wind, and usually fails to notice the net. Once the bird is caught, Arabian falconers only take some three or four weeks to train the bird for hunting which is very much faster than in Europe and other places.

Perhaps, too, mention should be made of that other adjunct to the sporting instincts of the desert man. The Saluqi, or Arabian Greyhound, is used for coursing hares and also for hunting gazelle, and is found in two races. One is quite short coated like

Falconry is still practised today by devotees utilising every detail of the old skills, as can be seen in the Wadi Dawasir (left).

its European cousin and the other has 'feathers' on its ears and tail. Both are naturally much smaller than Western greyhounds, and the former type was, at least some fifty years ago, predominantly to be found amongst the Mutayr, whilst the latter was kept by the 'Awazim. Whilst coursing for hares, the dogs are taught to quarter the ground some twenty or thirty yards apart and as many as half a dozen dogs are used at a time. When a hare is put up the dogs will run it down in the best coursing style. A similar principle is followed if gazelle are the quarry, though the hunting is often done with pairs or trios of dogs, and in this case it is interesting, and indeed wonderful, to see how from the start only one of the dogs follows the zigzag track of the fleeing gazelle. The others hang back and cut the corners. When the lead dog becomes tired its place is taken by one of the others. It is curious too that no one actually trains the dogs to do this. In effect, the dogs train each other. Indeed, older animals will knock back younger and inexperienced dogs who set off with enthusiasm to follow the zigzag line, until they learn how to pace themselves by cutting the corners.

Nature's Survivors

Flora

It is only to be expected that the flora of the desert cannot be described as rich. However, the plants and flowers which do occur seem to convey a sense of surprise and often give an impression of lushness in comparison to the barrenness of their surroundings.

Many desert plants are short lived annuals which evade the extremes of dessication and temperature by the formation of drought resistant seeds. Their main characteristics are rapid flowering and fruiting, springing into growth a few weeks after infrequent rain. Many of them have developed unusual chemical and physical means of measuring the amount of moisture available so that they can avoid germination if the rainfall is too scanty. Those plants which do live the year round have developed ways of reducing water loss by shedding leafage and other parts and suspending growth until water is available. The successful acacias have enormously long tap roots which reach subterranean water well out of the reach of other plants.

Most botanical families are represented and the constraints of the environment have frequently and interestingly produced many examples of convergent evolution with different plant species coming up with the same answer to the aridity problem. This can make identification difficult at times because without a flower the plants look very much alike.

Because of the shortage of plant life in the desert it is not surprising that what plants there are, have been exploited to the maximum degree by the bedouin inhabitants. There is not one that does not have some use other than the obvious one of fodder for domestic animals. The plants of the desert have all been pressed into service as sources of dyes for woven wool products, cosmetics and medicines for man and beast.

It is the acacia which is the most prominent feature of the desert flora. Two different species are quite common but the one most frequently met with is *Acacia tortilis* which has three or four small stalks in a group carrying the little leaves, whilst the other only has two. The flowers and leaves of both are protected by exceptionally sharp and dagger-like thorns which are not consumed with the leaves by the camel as some tales have it. The camel is able to use his prehensile lips to strip off the tender leaves without touching the thorns. *Acacia tortilis* flowers in the early summer and the second species, called *ehrenbergiana* blooms earlier in March and April. The leaves of both these acacias are beaten off the trees by the bedouin onto large round mats, and thus collected are used to feed small stock that either could not reach or would be unable to cope with the thorns. The tree is also much used for firewood and the manufacture of charcoal. Another large tree, which occurs as a single individual, rarely in groves, and situated in sheltered places with access to ground water, is the stately *ghaf* tree. It looks rather like an acacia but has no spines. Called *Prosopis cineraria* its elongated pods also provide fodder for animals, whilst its leaves were used instead of rice before this grain became available. Of the other larger plants the oleander is characteristic of the wetter wadis and though its bunches of pink flowers are attractive to look at the plant itself is very poisonous to animals. However, they seem to be able to avoid its bitter leaves and losses are rare due to this cause. Perhaps the most lush growth amongst the larger plants is the milkweed, *Calotropis*. It can grow to twelve feet or more and has large grey-green leaves. Once its wood was used to make the best charcoal for the manufacture of gunpowder. The plant produces a copious flow of white latex-like juice when cut. This contains toxic substances and was once used in some parts of the desert to cure camel mange.

Reduced leafage and a covering of fine hairs are the special characteristics of desert plants.

Eremobium lineare is a small crucifer which responds to the lightest rainfall.

Shiny leaves give protection to a plant by reflecting harsh sunlight.

Facing page: *This flower, like a Morning Glory, blooms only during the cool, early hours of the day. It is closed against the fierce heat within a couple of hours of sunrise.*

61

The most characteristic large trees of the desert are the acacias (top) and the ghaff (above). Both reach a great size, especially when they remain ungrazed. Each depends on a massive root system for survival.

The thorns of some species of acacia, known as samarah *in Arabic, provide very effective toothpicks.*

Acacias are protected by the small size of their leaves as well as a formidable armoury of thorns (see above). However, the thorns are no impediment to the camel, whose tongue is able to extract the leaves without any discomfort.

The oleander, left, is bright and decorative but is notoriously poisonous to animals.

Calotropis procera, *a member of the milkweed family is often found in lower wadi sides and outwashes. The plant is highly poisonous and much frequented by the butterfly* Danaus chrysippus *whose caterpillars utilise the poisonous juice of the plant to make themselves distasteful to predators. They advertise this fact with their gaudy stripes.*

The tamarisk grows in sandier and drier ends of wadi *outwashes. Normally it occurs in twiggy clumps, often up to twelve feet high. There are several species and some have very attractive flowers. The wood is quite hard grained and was often used in the past to make wooden bowls and other utensils.*

The picture at the top is of a plant from the attractively named Amaranth family. It is Aerva javanica and its woolly-textured stems and leaves form an admirable protection from dehydration. It is usually found in lowland districts. At one time it was used in villages of the Hijaz to stuff pillows and camel saddles.

The ubiquitous salt bush is shown above. When nothing else is available, camels will graze on this plant but it scours them badly. The plant's gelatinous leaves hold moisture and are a wonderful adaptation to the desert environment.

Gaillonia auchese, below, forms bushes up to about eight feet high in favourable conditions. In bloom, its frothy white flowers contrast strikingly with the dark stones of the wadi's edge. The hairiness of its felt-like leaves conserve the water content of the plant.

Above: *Arnebia decumbens prettily emphasises the use of hairs on the leaves to combat the aridity of a climate, whose average rainfall ranges between two and four inches a year.*

Left: *Leptadenia pyrotechnica shows how to survive with almost no leaves at all. The Arnebia has a reddish root which was once used as a cosmetic by bedouin women. Rubbed onto the face, it served as a very acceptable rouge.*

Cultivation of the date-palm has called for great resourcefulness in the arrangement of water supplies. The old systems of wells and water channels have been continuously replaced as more modern irrigation methods develop. Today, the Hofuf oasis is supplied with water in both quantity and quality unheard of only a few years ago.

However, the part played by plants in the story of man's conquest of the desert has not only been about his ability to exploit the wild flora. He has introduced many cultivated varieties of fruit and vegetable and grown them, often tenuously, in gardens whose defence from the encroaching desert has always been difficult. Perhaps the plant most famous in this respect is the date-palm, and its propagation has become the subject of much specialist knowledge. All date gardens are monuments to man's ingenuity, representing as they do very considerable feats of irrigation and engineering. Over the centuries many hundreds of different kinds have been developed and as the date-palm does not set seed which reproduces the perhaps special merit of the parent, propagation has to be effected by taking offshoots when they are two or three years old. Male and female flowers are borne on separate trees but offshoots are only taken from the female trees. A young palm will not produce more offshoots if all it has are taken away at once, so one or two are always left to encourage further growth. They are planted out in holes about a yard square and the same deep and some twenty feet apart. The trees do not need manuring and fertilizer to a great degree, but almost everywhere they do need irrigation. An interesting exception to this is found at Medina where the palms grow very successfully without it. Date palms bear fruit intermittently and older trees particularly like to rest every other year. Because very few male trees are grown, artificial pollination is necessary. This skill was developed many, many centuries ago and is the subject

Extensive agricultural research is taking place at Hofuf, where new and more prolific strains of date-palm are being introduced.

69

*The effects of failure in the irrigation system quickly become apparent.
As palms start to die, they show how dependent they are on man's
continued help. When this starts to happen, it often indicates a change
in the economic life of the community concerned.*

*Encroaching sand can quickly invade a garden, as can be seen, at
Jubail, top, in the Eastern Province.*

of ancient sculpture in Assyria and was accurately described by
Theophrastus. When the brush of male flowers covered by the
spathe has reached maturity, which can be determined both by
the scent and a very faint rustling produced by pressure of the
fingers, it is cut down and split open. One or two sprigs of these
male flowers, having been kept in a basket for a day, are pushed
into a cluster of female flowers which has just burst out of its own
spathe, which may also be artificially split. The operation is
carried out at mid-day in order to avoid possible damp.

The fruit of the palm has become a staple part of the diet of
the people of the area. It can be stored readily and the methods
employed in its preparation are legion. Dates are often picked
whilst still green when they are boiled for an hour or so and then
dried in the sun for about eight or nine days. They will then keep
for over a year. They can be pickled in vinegar and fresh dates can
be baked with butter or boiled in milk. Mixed with oils and
pounded, jams and sweets are made from them. The young male
spathes are used in salads or ground up to make bread and in the
Hijaz the stones themselves are soaked and ground to make
fodder for camels. Otherwise the palm produces valuable timber
for house construction and the leaves can be woven into mats.
The mid-ribs make useful supports for fencing and in some places
are even used to make small boats. The pith is edible, the fibre can
be utilized in rope making, and the leaves can also be used to
make a durable thatch.

Below: *Young palms are planted out in a new garden in the northern Hijaz.*

Left: *The palms themselves provide the materials which can be woven into fencing to protect a garden against wind-blown sand.*

Windbreaks of eucalyptus and casuarina stem the invading barchan dunes at the oasis of Al Hasa (left) in the Eastern Province. Such measures enable large new areas to be brought under cultivation.

In contrast to the small areas made possible by traditional methods, a small plot, below, lies in a side wadi *protected by an ancient dam which has silted up. As a result, there is almost total dependence on seasonal rainfall.*

A domed well, above, in Wadi Fatimah attests to an important aspect of water usage in the past. These structures were provided as a matter of charity along the major land routes.

The need to provide food and shelter for livestock is obvious and this attractive and traditional dove-cote in the Wadi Fatimah, above, is an interesting and unusual expression of this. It has a capacity for several hundred birds.

Fauna

The desert sustains a surprisingly rich fauna, both wild and domestic; but perhaps the most famous animal to be associated with both the desert country and its people is the camel. Its former importance for transport has been largely superseded by the motor truck and lorry, and it was used for this purpose throughout the Peninsula. As a riding animal the female is most usually employed. Camels were also used to pull carts and, either alone or in teams, to raise water from wells. However, many herds were maintained solely to provide milk, camel wool and meat. It is thus the most versatile domestic animal.

Camels can live for thirty to fifty years, being trained to carry loads in their third year though they do not usually perform regular work until their sixth. Retirement comes at about twenty-five. They are bred almost everywhere throughout the Peninsula but in Saudi Arabia the most important breeders are the 'Anayza in the north, the 'Utayba, Shammar, Qahtan and Dawasir tribes in mid-Arabia, and the Mutayr, 'Ajman, Dhafir and Murra in the east. Gestation takes thirteen months and it is almost invariable that no further mating is allowed for some ten or eleven months to enable the mother to regain her strength. A first calf is born in the sixth year of a camel's life; mating takes place during the period of December and January so that the calf is born a year after the following February or March, when it is fed on milk for about the first three months of its life. In some herds of milking camels when two females calve at about the same time, one of the calves is killed so that the remainder can take milk from both its own mother as well as a foster mother. During times of tribal migration the baby camels were often carried with the tribe's children on the backs of draught animals.

There are many quite specific breeds and the best have as much attention paid to their particular characteristics as do horses. A good female camel should be endowed with small and pointed ears and bright eyes. She should have a hard and arched neck carried strongly erect and muscular shoulders with wide well-fleshed hips and small feet. The breeds considered to be the best are named from their places of origin and are called Sharariya and Hutaymiya after the Hutaym and Shararat tribes, Tihiya after the Tih plateau in Sinai and Umaniya after Oman. The three pure breeds recognized in central Arabia are the somewhat shaggy Hurr breed produced by the 'Anayza and the Huwaytat, the 'Arqiyya of Bisha and Najran, and the Dara'iya of the south. In Hasa the Manasir possess a much praised light coloured breed called 'Usayfir. Each of these breeds has several strains each of which is suited to a particular terrain. In general those camels used for work on the gravel steppe are more heavily built than those used for work in the sands. It was usual for man and his animals to cover between twenty-five and thirty miles in a day's march whilst migrating, though riding camels can cover twice that distance. It is perhaps surprising today to realize how fast communications could be. For instance, with relays it was possible to reach Basra from Riyadh in only three days.

With the spring pasture camels can go for about two months without water, deriving their moisture needs solely from the new vegetation. In winter this invaluable characteristic to a desert dweller extends to a whole week. However, in the hot summer months they need to drink every three days.

The bedouin also exploits the sparse desert lands with donkeys of which there is a large white strain in Hasa, which is famous for producing excellent riding animals as well as strong pack animals. Crossed with good mares these animals also produce highly thought of mules. The Bedouin also relies on his flocks of sheep and goats of which there are many breeds and strains. Today, it is these rather than camels which provide his livelihood. The truck enables him to water flocks in a way hitherto considered impossible.

The camel is the animal associated in most people's minds with man's early exploitation of the desert.

It is not often realised what an important part the camel played in man's social development in the region. These beasts were not only the providers of milk, wool, meat and transport, they also performed a crucial role in the symbiosis between desert and cultivated areas. The huge herds of yesteryear were far more numerous than their potential as providers warranted. Their function was to act as objects of generosity so essential to the maintenance of a tribal leader's reputation. A reputation without which he would have found it impossible to keep his position. The prized camel thus attained a value far in excess of its material worth, simply because it could be given away.

The tradition of chivalry which the social aspect of the camel's past created is cherished today. Camel racing is one way in which this can be remembered and the superior expressions on the camels' faces as they run by a modern car give the impression that they are aware of former glories before the internal combustion engine replaced many of their functions.

Above: For four thousand years this has been the traditional picture of desert life. It expresses well the important part the camel has played in helping the Arab to overcome one of the most inhospitable regions of the world.

The Arabian oryx, Oryx leucoryx, *formerly found in large herds throughout the Peninsula, is a member of the antelope family and is superbly adapted to the desert environment.*

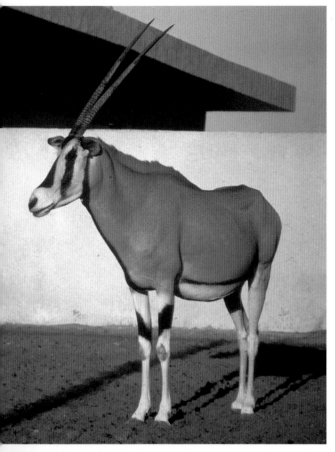

The gazelle is the most graceful of desert animals and there are three species to be found in the Peninsula. Like the oryx, it has suffered serious depletion in the past, but the Saudi government is actively preserving remaining stocks.

However, of all the domestic animals utilised by the bedouin it is the horse that provides the stuff of legend and story, romance and fable. The first half of this century saw a sad decline in horse-breeding which is now being reversed. This was due as much as anything to the introduction of firearms, whereas decline in camel breeding was due to the invention of the motor vehicle. Arab horses are justly famous throughout the world and apart from the role they played in warfare, where their speed enabled raiders to reach targets fast after a camel march, they were used to accompany Saluqi greyhounds on coursing expeditions, and in hunting with falcons. The tribes of the Arabian Desert most involved with breeding of horses were the Bani Khalid, Mutayr, Shammar, Dhafir, 'Anayza and the Murra. In the old days surplus animals would be exported to both India and Iraq as well as Egypt and Syria.

The best animals were produced on the steppes some two to three thousand feet above sea level and were much finer than those from the oases. The steppe horses were often thin but had the ability to recover condition quickly on the spring grazing which is often so abundant in the northern sands; and too, they developed an amazing endurance of thirst and hunger. It was common for a mare and her foal to cover over two thousand miles a year as they went with the tribal migrations. As a consequence of being trained to walk beside camels these animals develop a light springy step noted for its speed. Arab horses are also famous for their longevity, living on average about ten years longer than their European cousins.

Arabian horses are bred in all colours except black and piebald and the best descend from 'The Five', *al Khamsa*, which were chosen by the Prophet Muhammad. These five are called Kuhaylan, 'Ubbayyan, Saqlawi, Hamdani and Hadban and are the five progenitors of the five strains so named today. Naturally there are several hundred sub-strains but for all practical purposes three only are of importance at the present time. These remaining strains are the Kuhaylan, noted for strength and making ideal cavalry mounts and consisting in the main of greys; the Saqlawi which is the most refined and beautiful of Arab horses and the Mu'niqi, which is swifter and has longer, leaner lines than the other two.

It was usual for only mares to be ridden and most clans would only retain one stallion. Mares who produced filly foals were doted on by their owners and often fared better than the man's own family. They were wrapped in blankets to protect them from the cold and the mare's milk was supplemented with camel's milk. As gelding was not practised most colts were killed, particularly in hard years when poor grazing led to a shortage of camel's milk for the fillies and mares.

The wild fauna of the desert is not immediately obvious except for the gazelle which is largely nocturnal to avoid the heat of the day. Of the larger animals the gazelle is the one that is most frequently seen. There are two species, the Arabian gazelle proper which ranges over the gravel steppe and up through the wadis into the mountains; and the much more heavily built *rim* which is found in the sands. The oryx which is the size of a small donkey is now extinct but efforts to reintroduce this beautiful creature are proving successful. Its long straight horns are thought by some to be the origin of the story of the unicorn. The ostrich has, however, disappeared for good though its eggs can still be found as semi-fossils in the Empty Quarter. The cheetah, though probably never common, seems to have gone the way of the ostrich but may still maintain a foothold in very isolated areas of the desert. The leopard is usually confined to the lusher mountains in the south but occasional individuals may find their way out into the desert if there is good rainfall and consequently game can be had over a wider area. Hares are quite common and the desert abounds with mice of several different kinds which provide food

The Arabian horse we see today is largely a descendant of the wild horses recorded as originating in the south. At Dirab, below, invaluable work continues in preserving the qualities found in those horses from long ago.

for the jackals. The best place to see them is camped at night in the dunes. The wind blows grass seeds into a long line at the base of the dune and a torch will illuminate the feasting mice.

The desert birds are also fairly numerous but the main migration routes avoid the desert itself except in the coastal regions. Here is the source of falcons for sport, as the wild birds follow the flocks of migrating prey. This gives the trapper an opportunity to catch the falcons for training (as described above), though many are now imported.

Above: *The lop-eared sheep of the Hijaz is another animal entirely dependent on man for its survival. In effect, by assisting man it has ensured its own survival.*

Overleaf: *A flock of birds wheel and swoop over a desert pool near Laylah.*

Arabian fauna is rich in reptilian life and no part of the desert, mountain or wadi is without a representative of this highly successful group. They have played no part in man's exploitation of the arid lands but have rather survived alongside him. In general, man has only been able to use some of the skins. However, the tail of the large spiny-tailed lizard can be eaten and tastes very much like chicken.

Above: *The Arabian Toad-Headed Agama,* Phynocephalus arabicus, *can bury itself very quickly by wriggling energetically.*

The grasshopper, right, is more suited in appearance to dark crevices, unlike its cousin, facing page, *whose coloration is more appropriate to open spaces.*

84

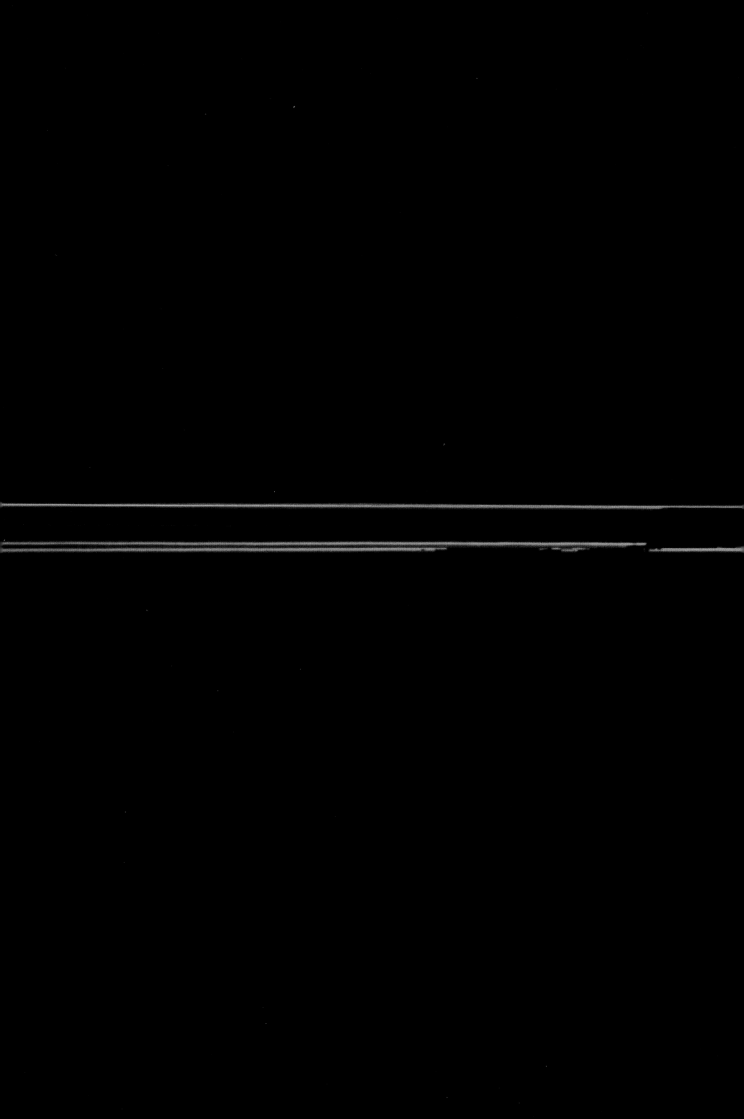

The Advance of Technology

The society of man that doggedly flourished in the desert and supported itself by exploiting these, perhaps, simple animal and vegetable resources has, in the twentieth century, become caught up in the story of the industrial development of the rest of mankind. Until the nineteenth century man's needs for lubricating and lighting oils had been satisfied by animal and vegetable oils. However, by the nineteenth century these were no longer sufficient for the spate of mechanical inventions which had been responsible for the Industrial Revolution. The whaling industry developed at an enormous rate and the whales themselves were almost exterminated in the frantic search to maintain oil supplies to growing industries. In any case these oils were themselves inadequate in quality for the kinds of machines that were being developed. In fact this development was itself being retarded for the lack of suitable lubricants. The first milestone in the story of the forthcoming changes was the discovery of a way to distil lamp oil from coal. This took place in 1850. At this time petroleum collected from natural springs was only used for medicinal purposes, though attempts were being made to find other commercial uses for it. It is amusing today to think that contamination with petroleum was a common complaint of the salt water well industry in the United States where it was regarded as a serious nuisance. However in 1859 a well was drilled in Pennsylvania specifically for the purpose of finding oil by a group of people who had faith that there was a good commercial use for the product. Such was the tiny beginning of what has become the largest industry in the world.

After the initial discovery there was a mad scramble as the oil was found to have so many uses. The multiplicity of uses encouraged the development of more machinery and the demand, feeding on itself, created more uses still. However, it was the development of the internal combustion engine which created a demand for huge quantities of oil. So colossal became the demand that it was necessary for the industrialising nations to search throughout the world for more and more sources of a material that had become the very lifeblood of their development and prosperity. In the early thirties the eyes of the explorers were turned to the Middle East and not a few looked at the deserts of Arabia. To begin with all sides conducted the necessary negotiations with a mixture of desperate faith and forlorn hope. Europe and the United States were emerging from the financial desert of the Depression and legislation by their own governments created difficulties in both making and maintaining payments. However, a concession agreement was signed in 1933 and the momentous events were set in train that were to lead to, if not the conquest, then at least the subduing of the desert itself.

The benefits of wealth in the barren desert lands have transformed them from lands where very survival was a fierce struggle against nature to lands of promise and ease. The ways that man himself had forged down the centuries to succeed in the hard environment of the desert no longer seem appropriate, and every new road emphasises the changes that are taking place. The wonders of technology have altered man's life throughout the world and everywhere the questioning arising from them and their assimilation has led to enormous changes in human society. So it is with the desert; but the formidable traits of endurance and the form of society created by the desert will not disappear like a tent of yesterday blown away in the sandstorm.

Oil rig wild-catting at Al Minhal (right) in the northern Rub' al Khali signposts the way to modern Arabia.

Previous pages: *On the busy road between Riyadh and Dammam, nocturnal traffic and a gas flare at Abqaiq attest to the pace at which development is taking place.*

Western man has become so expert in exploiting natural resources that he has come to take them for granted, and, not reckoning the changes his technology has brought to him, rarely considers their effect on others. The consequence is an unconscious arrogance and lack of humility. Deserts do move one to philosophy and are places where for centuries and aeons of time the arrogance of nature has taught mankind much humility. Today we are able to so protect ourselves from the full rigours of the desert so that the stories of the old life, the tales of hardship and suffering, almost seem a fairy-tale. It is as though we are losing our sense of proportion. An old bedu pithily restored the balance when a satellite was pointed out to him crossing the huge desert sky. It was described to him as being a wonderful example of technology and he gazed at it for a while, displaying no incredulity or admiration whatever. He then just remarked that he thought it was rather useless. It moved far too fast to steer by and he thought he would stick to the stars already provided by God.

Survey helicopters in the Rub' al Khali (above), an oil rig on gypsum (far left) and a light aircraft crossing the dunes are just a few of the tools with which modern man has finally overcome the hitherto impregnable barriers of the desert.

The first rigs were permanent structures (see right) and could not be moved from site to site. Today these skeletons chart man's progress across the Peninsula, unlike the mobile unit shown above.

Above: *A blow-out aflame is every oilman's nightmare and is a terrifying example of nature's power when subterranean oil and gas break out of control. Almost seven hundred feet of flame roar out of the earth in seconds and toast can be made half a mile away. The gas flare at Abqaiq (left) seems tame by comparison which, indeed, it is.*

This pipeline in the Dahna (below) *carries crude from the oilfields to the refinery in Riyadh.*

Above: *A sand storm gathers momentum in the dusk near Qaisumah where the Tapline*   *snakes towards the Mediterranean Sea from the oil fields in the east of the Peninsula.*

Above: *On the road to Hofuf, serene outcrops survey a frenetic network of pipelines while a 'Christmas Tree' (left), the name given to the final well-valve, ironically contrasts with the immensity of its setting.*

As crude oil is released from confinement
below ground, great structures and complex
technology are required to transport it to the
refineries. Man's ingenuity in devising systems
to gather and pump the oil across vast
distances is displayed in these installations in
the Eastern Province (top, above & right).

Exploration and extraction are but two aspects of the oil business in the Arabian Peninsula. Much of the crude is refined within its borders to meet not only domestic requirements, but to feed diverse oil-dependent enterprises which range from agriculture, pharmaceuticals and electronics to synthetic fibres, plastics and transportation. The refinery at Jeddah (above & left) is part of this chain.

At Hofuf (top), Jeddah (centre) and Dhalam (above), rock crushing plants and cement *factories provide, visually, a stark contrast to the surrounding landscape.*

Oil has not only produced a rich harvest of products for the amelioration of man's lot. It has also created other consequential needs within the Peninsula. Not least among these is the generation of an infrastructure requiring vast quantities of construction materials, of which cement is an integral ingredient.

The Hajj Terminal at Jeddah Airport is a testament to the achievements of modern Arabia and blends harmoniously with established traditional shapes.

The pylons, above, seem to almost dance across the landscape, bringing power to both the cities and remotest villages.

These pages demonstrate various aspects of the Kingdom's road network. The busy Riyadh-Dammam road (right) *hums with traffic both day and night.*

Previous pages: *The tortuous bends on the descent from Tayif to Makkah give a graphic portrait of the natural obstacles to be overcome in establishing a modern infrastructure.*

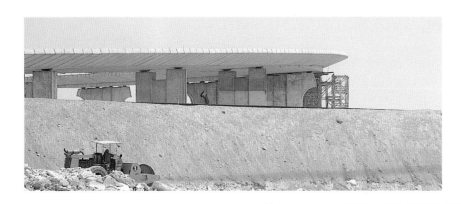

The truck, below, illustrates the growth in trade that the new roads have made possible. At the same time, it gives a stark reminder of what it must have been like to take a camel train through conditions such as these.

Modern transport has functions other than those which are purely connected with trade. It enables people, who have been separated for centuries, to mix together in ways that were impossible in earlier times.

It is a poignant comment on the Arab genius that, far from being swamped by Western technology, the people have adapted traditional patterns and arabesques to decorate their powerful trucks.

Left: This large traffic interchange in the Eastern Province is just one small part of the extensive road network which criss-crosses the Peninsula.

About thirty or forty years ago, it took weeks and months to get a letter out of central Arabia and as long again to send a reply back. Today, it is possible to communicate with all quarters of the globe almost instantly. The microwave station near Abqaiq, below, is part of one of the most sophisticated telecommunications systems in the world.

The solar powered telephone (left), beside the road north of Medina, is another example of modern technology helping to reduce the awesome proportions of the desert.

The creation of a transport network has always been at the forefront of man's increasingly successful attempts to control his environment. The Hijaz Railway, right & opposite, used to link Medina with the countries to the north.

The rail network which connects Riyadh with the busy port of Dammam, in the Eastern Province, is equipped with powerful diesel locomotives such as the one pictured at Hofuf (above).